The Courageous Parent

A selection of Adlerian child-rearing techniques to help parents raise responsible, cooperative children

**Cindy Walton-McCawley, M.Ed.
Kathleen A. Walton**

Published by:

Adlerian Child Care Books, 1313 St. Andrews Rd. Columbia, SC 29210

Copyright 2009 by Cindy Walton-McCawley and Kathleen A. Walton

ISBN-13   978-0-615-29833-7
ISBN-10   0-6152-9833-8

Table of Contents

Foreword

In this book you will find techniques designed to help parents of children from birth to 11 years of age to meet some of the most common child rearing challenges. Each of the suggestions is based upon the Individual Psychology of Alfred Adler, or Adlerian Psychology which was originally introduced in North America by Adler's colleague, psychiatrist Rudolf Driekurs. All of the techniques have been used successfully by parents of students enrolled in Adlerian based programs. In fact, the child rearing practices you are about to read were specifically developed as a resource for the parents of students in Adlerian Child Care Centers, Inc. Adlerian Child Care Centers has five child development centers and three after school enrichment programs in Columbia, South Carolina. The centers have been in operation since 1974. The techniques came about in response to requests for child rearing approaches by parents of students enrolled in the centers.

We hope you find the child rearing practices helpful with your own child or with those parents you are attempting to help. Having a repertoire of sound parenting techniques is crucial to raising responsible and cooperative children. It is equally important to understand the theory behind the parenting techniques. By having a child rearing philosophy, parents are more likely to keep their parenting styles consistent. Toward that end, an overview of Adlerian Psychology has been provided. It has been our experience that parents who have a good understanding of Individual Psychology and child rearing techniques based upon Adlerian principles are better equipped to succeed in raising caring, cooperative and responsible children.

Overview of Adlerian Psychology

Alfred Adler is the founder of Individual Psychology, or Adlerian Psychology. His theory is one of practicality and good common sense. Adlerian Psychology offers parents a guide towards understanding how they can help their child to develop responsible, cooperative behaviors. It offers parents a guide for helping their child to develop behaviors that are in the interest not only of the child, but also in the interest of society. All individuals develop a style and a pattern that serves them in meeting the challenges of social living. From an Adlerian perspective, behavior is best interpreted from a holistic point of view: there is a unity to one's approach to life with a style and pattern that the individual develops. That style and pattern, also known as lifestyle, is developed at a very young age. Understanding what influences the development of lifestyle better equips parents to raise their children to be responsible, caring and contributing members of society.

A good place to start when seeking to understand children's development is the principle that all individuals are motivated to belong, or to feel connected to society. When a child comes into the world, he looks for clues and messages that he belongs to the social group in which the child finds himself. The first place this occurs is the family. Often this is where well intentioned and loving parents make the first mistakes. Take for example the newborn infant that comes home with Mom and Dad from the hospital. The parents are overjoyed with their baby. They coo and love their infant, feed the child and change the child's diaper. It is now time for the infant to sleep. The parents have lovingly prepared a $3,000.00 nursery that could be photographed for a home décor magazine. The parents place the child into his crib. The child begins to cry. The parents, concerned that their child is distressed, pick him up from his crib. They attempt to console the child. They place him back in his crib. The infant begins to cry. The parents take the child out of his crib in an attempt to pacify him. This is repeated several times until the parents give up and bring the infant into their room. The $3,000.00 nursery goes unused. The child has been sent a clear message or clue on how he belongs in the family. When a problem occurs, the infant can cry and Mom or Dad, or both, will come and solve it for him.

The principle of belongingness or social embeddedness is a key towards understanding children's behavior. All individuals seek to find a way to belong in society. The first place children look to belong is the family, followed by the preschool, elementary school, secondary schools and so on into adulthood. Parents and educators of young children sometimes send messages and clues to children that lead them to feel they are not significant members of their family and schools. While belongingness is one of the easiest principles of Adlerian Psychology to understand, it seems to be one of the most difficult for parents and educators to use effectively. If one asks parents and educators what character traits they would hope to see children develop, the following list typically results: responsible, cooperative, kind, able to problem solve, intelligent. The survey would find that people typically want the same things for their children.

Unfortunately, while parents and educators of young children have very similar values, they often spend more time with negative behaviors, than with pro-social behaviors. This leads to a mixed message. When children engage in uncooperative behaviors, the typical response of a parent is to spend time correcting the child. Bear in mind the following; "That which we attend to is what we will see again and again." If parents spend their time addressing misbehavior, they will see it repeated.

The infant who cries when placed in his crib to sleep is looking for a message on how to solve the problem. The message that his parents sent in the previous example is one of discouragement. Faced with solving the problem of going to sleep in his crib, the infant discovers that by crying he is excused from solving the problem and he succeeds at getting his parents involved with him. The infant's crying helped him to find a way to belong. Were the parents to be asked if this is the behavior they want from their infant, they would reply, "No, we want our baby to sleep." The actions of the parents actually run counter to what they want for their baby. The parents responded to the crying rather than having the courage to allow their infant to learn to sleep in his crib. It is a frequent mistake made by parents to spend time and energy with children when they are engaged in misbehavior rather than when children are being cooperative. It can be corrected if parents take a step back from misbehavior and ask themselves, "Is this the behavior that I want to see again and again?" When we take a step back, we allow children to learn how to solve a problem independently.

An equally important principle of Adlerian Psychology is that all individuals strive for superiority or perfection. Simply put, this means that no one will stand to be in a position of inferiority. If a person senses herself to be in a minus position, whether this is real or imagined, she will seek to move toward what she perceives to be a plus position. Suppose for a moment that a four year old has just tied her shoe for the first time. The child sees her Mother and holds out her foot to show Mother her accomplishment. The mother looks at the shoe and says, "You tied your shoe! You did a pretty good job, but let me tie it tighter for you because it looks like it may come loose." As Mother bends down to retie the shoelace, the child's face falls. The next time the child's shoes need tying, she asks her Mother to tie them.

While Mother meant to help her child, she actually discouraged the child from learning to tie her shoe on her own. When the child performed the action on her own, Mother's message to her child was that the child had made a mistake. What could have been a positive action instead became a negative one. Rather than be told that she does not measure up to mother's standards the child chooses to let mother continue to tie her shoes. The child, not wanting to be placed in a position of inferiority, makes Mother into a servant. This is what is referred to as the imagined plus. Shoe tying met with discouragement and being placed in a position of inferiority. Letting Mother tie the shoes means that Mom has to do the work and the child does not risk being told what a poor job she did.

While Mother believes that she has helped her child, she has actually done the exact opposite. This results from a misunderstanding of the basic principle that people will not stand to be placed into a position of inferiority. When children sense themselves to be in a minus position they will find a way to move into a plus position. In the example above, the child elects not to tie her shoe rather than risk being told by Mother that she has performed poorly. The far better response on Mother's part would have been to say, "You tied your shoe! Can you show me how you did that?" This paves the way for the child to demonstrate her new skill to her mother. Mother should say nothing about the loosely tied shoes. Let the natural consequence of the shoelace coming untied occur. When it does, let the child solve the problem on her own by tying the shoe tighter.

A third basic principle of Adlerian Psychology is that behavior is goal directed and purposeful. People engage in behavior that is useful to them. When a child senses himself to be in an encouraging environment where opportunities for taking responsibility occur, he will develop responsible and cooperative behaviors. However, when a child meets with discouragement and senses that life is somehow out of his control, he is likely to use misbehavior to compensate for feelings of inferiority in an attempt to find a way to belong. In young children this misbehavior occurs in one of four directions: attention, power, revenge and inadequacy. They are referred to as the four mistaken goals of behavior. The most frequently used mistaken goals of behavior are attention and power. Of those two, attention is the most frequently seen goal of misbehavior. Attention seeking behavior results from a child drawing the conclusion that he or she is only significant when he or she is being talked with or served by parents. A prime example of this can occur in households during the morning routine.

The parents wake up and Dad walks into his son's room and gently wakes up his child. He rubs the child's head saying, "Time to get up and get dressed for school." Dad leaves the room and goes to get dressed. His son rolls over and goes back to sleep. Mom comes into the room ten minutes later and says, "Honey, it's time to get up." She gently pulls her son out of bed and sits him up. She leaves the room and in another ten minutes returns to the room to find her son sitting where she left him. She helps her son get dressed and then carries him down to the kitchen where Dad has prepared a bowl of cereal for the child. Dad says, "Eat up son; we have to get to school, put your bowl in the sink when you are done." The child slowly eats his cereal. When he is finished, he sits complacently at the table. Dad says, "Look at the time, we've got to go!" Mom responds, "I'll take care of clean up, you two need to head out. Have a good day!" Dad grabs his son's book bag, he and his boy get into the car, and Dad drives the child to school. Mom cleans up from breakfast and then hurries to work herself. Their son, age 5, heads in to kindergarten having been dressed, served and cleaned up after by his parents.

The example above, all too familiar in many homes, helps to illustrate how the well-intentioned, but misguided parents play into the child's mistaken goal of attention and service. Both parents spoke very frequently with their child. They also both provided services for their child that he could perform on his own. The child is excused from responsible and cooperative behavior. The child arrives at school with the misguided notion that the rest of the world is here to serve him. It is not a great leap of faith to imagine the problems that the child will encounter in school where he is one of 20 students and the teacher is not able to meet his every need. Unless the parents change their parenting approach, the crown prince is set up for failure.

Attention and service seeking behaviors on the part of a child are useful if the child is successful at getting people to talk unnecessarily with him or to do for the child what he could do for himself. The child has mistakenly concluded that he is only worthwhile when he is the center of attention, or getting service. These children are ill prepared for the give and take of life.

The second most prevalent mistaken goal of behavior is power. When demonstrating her power, the child is attempting to show parents that she will not be made to do things. One example that helps illustrate this is cleaning up toys. In many households, the parent mistakenly believes she can make the child clean up her toys. The parent asks the child to clean up her room so they can go to the store. After about ten minutes the parent returns to the child's room to discover the child is still playing with her toys. The parent says to the child, "I told you to clean up your room and I meant it. Now get this room cleaned up!" The child half-heartedly begins to clean up. The parent leaves the room and the child returns to her play. The parent checks on the child a little while later to find the child back at play and the room not cleaned. The parent angrily says, "That's it young lady! Clean up this room now! I'm not leaving until you do!" The child sullenly cleans up the room with the parent standing guard.

In a power struggle a fight is taking place between parent and child. From the parent's perspective, the issue is having a child clean her room. From the child's perspective the issue is to demonstrate to her parent that she won't be controlled or forced to do things. While the parent succeeded at forcing the child to clean her room, the child has won the battle. She has succeeded in drawing the parent into a fight and has even taken a hostage. By refusing to clean up without the direct supervision of the parent, the child is in control of when she and her parent will go to the store.

The third goal of misbehavior is revenge. While it is not as common a mistaken goal as attention and power, revenge certainly presents tremendous challenges for parents and early childhood educators. The child who misbehaves in the direction of revenge is likely to have drawn the conclusion that he is disliked, hated or at least is being treated unfairly and feels hurt. He can decide he is entitled to hurt others. Children using this goal engage in behaviors that are designed to physically or psychologically hurt their parents. These children may routinely break the parent barrier. In other words, they will hit, scratch, kick or bite parents, and quite likely will do the same to friends and teachers. When they believe themselves to be wronged they feel entitled to make others feel hurt. A snapshot of a household with a child using revenge might look something like this. Two brothers, ages 4 and 2, are playing together while their mother is preparing dinner. The younger child grabs a toy from his older brother. The older brother screams at his brother, "That's mine! Give it back!" and grabs back the toy. The younger child begins crying. Mother, observing the scenario, says to the older child, "Your brother is little, he just wants to play too. Give him back the toy." The older brother refuses saying, "But they're my toys!" Mother persists and yells, "I said to give your little brother the toy! I am sick of your selfishness!" The older sibling takes the toy and throws it in his younger brother's face. The 2 year old begins crying hysterically; Mother rushes over and grabs her older son, pulling him away from the two year old. The older son kicks his mother and yells, "I hate you! I hate all of you!" The older brother, feeling he is being treated unfairly and unkindly, has chosen to hurt others back in a misguided effort to right the scales. None of the parties involved have engaged in friendly, cooperative or responsible behaviors and the result is hurtful to all of the family.

The fourth goal of misbehavior is to display inadequacy in order to avoid failure. Inadequacy is not so easily identified because the misbehavior is often not recognized. With inadequacy, the mistaken logic on the part of the child might be phrased as "No matter what I do, I fail. Better to do nothing rather than risk failure." Children engaged in the goal of inadequacy may appear to be apathetic, or to be daydreamers. In fact, the daydreaming or apathy is the misbehavior that they often employ to avoid risking failure. The discouragement comes from a well-intentioned parent, but one who has failed to communicate to the child that the child can handle the tasks of life. In this household, a child is often held up to unrealistic expectations by a well meaning, but overly ambitious or perfectionistic parent. Consider the following example. A 3 year old is poured a cup of juice by Dad and carries it to the table. Along the way the child drops the cup of juice, which spills. Dad exclaims, "Honey! I've told you to use both hands when you are carrying your juice. Now look at the mess." The child begins to cry. Dad cleans up the spill saying, "I'll get another cup when I clean up your spill." He then pours the child another cup of juice saying, "Here you go, now hold it with both hands." The child does not take it. Dad says, "Okay, you go sit in the chair and I'll put your juice on the table." Dad leads his daughter to a chair where she sits down and he places the cup in front of her. The unspoken message to the child is that making a mistake means she is a failure. Faced with the discouraging message that she is a failure, the child elects not to carry the cup at all. At least by not carrying her cup, she does not risk being told that she does not measure up. In a short period of time, should Dad continue to focus on his daughter's shortcomings rather than his daughter's successes, the child is at risk for deciding no action is better than risking being told she is a failure.

Parenting styles can contribute positively or negatively to children's behavior. There are three common approaches to parenting. They are pampering, coercion, and democratic. The first two, pampering and coercion, are troublesome approaches to child rearing.

Pampering is one of the most common mistakes made by parents. When parents routinely do for a child what the child could do for himself, they are pampering the child. This takes place far too frequently because parents mistakenly believe they are helping their child. There is a great price paid for pampering because when parents pamper, they steal from their child the courage to solve problems independently. The pampering parent excuses his child from the give and take that is called for in life. It is not uncommon to hear the pampering parent make excuses for his child. In essence, pampering a child weakens him. Children who are pampered learn to rely on others to solve their problems. One of the greatest gifts parents can give to their children is to stand back and let children learn to master tasks and solve problems on their own. When parents do this, they are indicating to their children that they believe their children can handle the challenges that life presents. This is very difficult for the pampering parent and while the parent means well, he is in fact hindering a child from developing responsible and cooperative behaviors.

The other mistaken approach to parenting is coercion. Parents using coercion are trying to force or make their child behave or cooperate. In the coercive or authoritarian household a state of war often exists. The parent is actually engaged in a fight with the child over her behavior and the child decides to fight back or resist the parent. This can result in a power struggle between the parent and child. While the parent may succeed in forcing a child to conform, it is at a great cost to the child's ability to develop into a cooperative and responsible individual. When children sense themselves to be controlled, they often will decide to rebel. This rebellion can be active, as in the case of tantrums and open refusal to accede to a parent's demands. It can also be passive as in the case of stubbornness. In households where it is not safe to resist openly, children may quietly refuse to cooperate. A common example of this is the child who a parent is trying to toilet train. The parent forces the child to sit on the toilet in a misguided attempt to toilet train the child. The child refuses to produce while on the toilet. After returning to play, the child soils her clothes. The unspoken message from the child is simple, "You will not control me." Sulking, pouting and stubbornness are not uncommon behaviors. In the coercive household, cooperation and self-reliance are not taught. Rather, the parent is looking for compliance. The child, sensing herself to be in a position of inferiority without control over her life, can seek to right the perceived injustice by refusing to cooperate or to engage in responsible behaviors.

The third approach to parenting is democratic. In this approach, parents look for opportunities to deliberately encourage behaviors that are helpful to the child as well as to the societies in which the child belongs: family, preschool and school. When misbehavior occurs, the parent uses techniques designed to stop the usefulness of the misbehavior. Parents avoid the pitfalls of blame, they side step power struggles. They do not do unnecessary talking, and they do not provide unnecessary service. Parents allow their child to learn from his mistakes and to discover the natural and logical consequences of misbehavior. They do not excuse their child from his misbehavior, but neither do they dwell upon it as that might make the misbehavior useful to the child. Responsibility is taught by parents who give children responsibility rather than by demanding it. Cooperation and kindness are taught by parents who spend time interacting with their child when he is being kind and cooperative. Democratic parents introduce respect for others into the child's life. They take advantage of opportunities to spread the child's interest to include Mother, Father, other members of the family and other members of society.

All individuals have the potential to develop social interest. The socially interested child finds ways to successfully meet the challenges of life that are a help to the child as well as society. Parents directly influence the development of social interest in their child. Parents want to use child rearing strategies and techniques that help their child to become a caring, responsible, and contributing member of society. Adlerian psychology provides parents with a framework in which they can accomplish this. In the words of Dr. Frank Walton, an internationally renowned Adlerian psychologist, "The job of a parent is to work themselves out of a job by the time a child is eighteen years of age."

When the principles above are put together it becomes clear that children (all individuals in fact) want to belong and feel that they are contributing members of the social settings in which they find themselves. Children want to move from minus positions to plus positions. When children are discouraged, or made to feel that they are not worthwhile, they will attempt to compensate for real or imagined feelings of inferiority with behaviors that they mistakenly believe help them to belong and feel superior. The misbehaving child is a discouraged child. The task of the parents of a misbehaving child is two-fold.

First, they must use child rearing techniques that stop the use of the child's misbehavior.

Secondly, they need to deliberately encourage socially interested behavior, i.e. concern for fellow human beings.

In this book parents will find many techniques designed to stop the use of children's misbehavior. They will also find techniques designed to deliberately encourage children's cooperation skills, self reliance, concern for others and independence. While both types of techniques are important, only deliberate encouragement has the potential to teach a child socially interested behaviors. When both types of techniques are used together, a child who is engaging in misbehavior will come around to cooperative and responsible behaviors more quickly. The techniques that follow are designed to help parents meet that goal.

The Role of Birth Order in the Family

The order in which children are born into their families has an impact on their development. While each individual has their own private logic it is not uncommon to see children in similar birth order positions draw similar conclusions. While birth order in and of itself does not determine a child's personality development, it does affect it. Understanding potential influences of birth order positions can provide parents with insight into possible areas of strengths and weaknesses in their children. Some psychologists believe that birth order is the single most influential factor in personality development.

To understand birth order influences, it is important for parents to realize that we are speaking of psychological birth order. Keep in mind that if there is a five year or more interval between children, we typically see the start of a new group in the family. Thus, if a family has a twelve year old, a six year old, and a four year old, the twelve year old is likely to have more of the characteristics of an only child. The six year old may have more of the characteristics of a first born since he is the first of the second group, while the twelve year old has six important years living as an only child.

The characteristics below are often found in children who have the following birth order positions.

The only child in a family can be introspective, imaginative and different. She is not typically rule conscious, although she typically identifies with the values of the parents. Remember, rules necessary for a family of four children will vary greatly for a family with one child. She may be confident and comfortable with adults and older children. Remember, the only child grows up in a world of adults. She may experience pressure from parents to be successful as she is the only "standard bearer" for the family. She may be demanding and have challenges with sharing. The only child does not have to share the attention of her parents. The only child can be a loner and does enjoy time spent alone. In a room filled with noise and other children, the only child may look for a quiet place to play. Parents of only children will want to create opportunities for their child to experience sharing and social interaction with other children her age. The only child can benefit from learning she cannot always have her way.

The first born, or oldest child, tends be responsible and assertive. He often likes to be the leader. He can be bossy. He is attuned to rules and may be a conformist. First born children may be the "junior Mommy" or "junior Daddy" in the household. Remember that their first family models were their parents. Before they were oldest children, for a brief period of time they were only children. First born children can make good leaders. They may struggle with being followers. Parents of first born children will want to balance recognizing their child's leadership skills with teaching them the skills of cooperation. If the family is playing a game together, avoid letting your oldest child decide on the game each time. Every first born child experiences "dethronement" upon the birth of the second child. This does not necessarily mean that he feels passed by, but it does mean that the first born must decide what to make of the life experience. Many first born children will decide to become Mom or Dad's little helper. While the first born child may be happy to be Mommy's little helper, it is equally important for the other children in the family to have the same opportunity. At some point it may be valuable to say to your oldest child, "I know you like to help and I appreciate it. I also need to make sure that your brothers and sisters learn how to do this as well. Thank you for giving them the chance to learn."

The second born child is often competitive. She observes the first born and strives to catch up to him or her. The second child tends to be thoughtful, creative, social and more of a risk taker. She may also develop into a rebel. The second born arrives in the family and finds her place based upon the place that the first born has made for his or her self. Like the first born, the second born looks for a way to belong in the family that is significant. It is not unusual to find that the second born child is very different from the first born child. The second born will find a different way to belong to the family than the first born. Parents of a second born child can encourage their child by staying clear of comparing them to the oldest child. The second born child is often a champion of the underdog.

A middle born child requires the presence of at least three children in the family. He can be concerned with fairness and usually avoids conflict. He can be a peacekeeper. The middle child will be the first child to let you know if he got the smallest glass of juice. The middle child is usually cooperative and easy going. The middle child can be a team player and works well with others. In the interest of avoiding conflict, the middle child can have trouble voicing his opinion. Sometimes the middle child can feel he is overlooked. Parents of middle children can help them by letting them choose what game might be played or which story should be read. Since middle children are often second born, they may have some characteristics of the second born.

The last born or youngest child in the family is often humorous and sensitive. They can be helpless or insecure. They are usually playful, athletic and do not shy away from drawing attention to themselves. They are comfortable being in the center stage position. The youngest child may have time management challenges if other members of the family serve as their timekeepers. The youngest child may also develop into the baby of the family. In some families, the youngest child is referred to by family members as the baby. The other family members provide so much service to the baby, that she is robbed of the opportunity to develop responsible and self-reliant behaviors. Parents of youngest children serve their child well by letting the youngest child learn to master tasks just as they did with their older children. Care must also be taken not to let the older children do for the youngest child what she can do for herself. Youngest children who are not overly pampered frequently make extraordinary achievements in life due to their wish to avoid being last and the unusual perspective of being able to learn from the successes and difficulties of older siblings.

The Family Meeting

The family meeting, or family council, is an excellent tool for uniting the family. Family meetings help children learn how they can contribute to the family. The family council allows family members to work together to solve problems, plan outings and share their thoughts on what is going well in the family. Children as young as three can take part in family meetings.

To get your family meetings started, decide on a set meeting time at which everyone can be present and is willing to be present. Meetings should not exceed twenty minutes. For the first meeting, after thanking everyone for gathering, say, "Your Dad and I thought it would be helpful if we got together as a family once a week to see how we are doing and what each of us could do to help out the family. Anything from planning a family event, to solving a household problem, or just letting each other know how one of us helped out could be discussed in our meeting. Whatever we decide upon in our meetings will be put to a vote. If everyone is in agreement, we will use the idea, if not, then we won't use the idea. Does this sound okay to everyone?"

In a respectful way, you need to set up the ground rules for the meetings. They are as follow:

We take turns speaking.
Everyone gets one vote.
Votes must be unanimous, or no action is taken.
No one may speak unkindly.
Suggestions for the meeting can be written down in the family meeting log for future meetings.

Once meeting rules have been established, we suggest using the first meeting for planning a family outing and addressing a household issue that needs a quick fix. For example, have the family decide whether they would like to go to the zoo or have a picnic in the park in the near future. Allow each family member to offer their ideas about which activity they would like to do. Initial meetings will need chairing by a parent; however, to encourage leadership and discussion skills, let children take turns leading the meeting in the future. Once the discussion surrounding the family outing has come to a close, take a vote on the outing. It is important that votes be unanimous. If there is a dissenting vote, don't be overly concerned. Say to the family members, "It seems that we cannot agree on what we want to do. How about if we give this some thought over the next week and we can meet again to see if we can come to an agreement?" This gives the dissenters the opportunity to change their vote rather than have no family outing, and it is encouraging for them to learn that they are not going to have decisions forced upon them. If there is no agreement, table the issue until the next meeting.

The next item on the agenda should be simple. While addressing all the household chores may be tempting, it is not a realistic goal. Remember, meetings should not exceed 20 minutes. You might try asking family members for their ideas on how to solve the nightly task of setting the table. Again, whatever solutions are presented must come to a vote. If there is disagreement, the meeting chair can ask that person if he or she would be willing to try the suggestion for one week and report back at the next meeting whether he or she is willing to continue with the suggestion or not. If there is no agreement, parents can say, "Since we cannot agree for now, we will work on a solution for the next meeting." Use the next week to demonstrate how cooperation is a two way street. When it's time to set the table, ask the children to help set the table. If they are unwilling, Mom and Dad can get their plates and let the children work out the problem of getting their places set. From the chaos, the children will come to understand that there is a need for order. By letting them see the consequences of uncooperative behavior, they will realize that they need to work together to solve the problem. They can learn that every man and woman for his or her self is not a very attractive practice in family life. By the next meeting, they will no doubt have several suggestions for nightly table setting.

While the family council cannot solve all family issues, it can certainly solve many of them. Used regularly, the family council helps every member of the family feel he or she has a say in how the family operates. It paves the way for family members to help one another for a common cause, namely, the good of the family.

Home Responsibilities for Children

The best way to teach children responsible behavior is by giving children responsibilities. By allowing children to lend a hand with simple tasks, we send the message to them that we believe they are capable. This can start as young as age two. Listed below are tasks and self help skills that children can perform as well as the age at which they can be expected to do them.

Two Year Olds
1. Picks up toys and puts in proper place.
2. Places books and magazines in a book bin or bookshelf.
3. Clears dishes from the table and places on the counter. Puts napkin in the trash.
4. Cleans up spills.
5. Selects from two breakfast foods to make a simple decision.
6. Toilet training.
7. Performs simple personal hygiene tasks such as washing and drying hands and face, brushing teeth and hair.
8. Pulls comforter up over bed to assist with making bed.
9. Puts dirty clothes in clothes hamper.
10. Carries school bag into and out of child development center.
11. Undresses and dresses with some help.
12. Puts jacket on by self.

Three Year Olds
1. Dresses independently with exception of tying shoes.
2. Assists with setting the table for meals.
3. Makes a simple dessert. Adds topping to cupcakes, whipped cream on pudding.
4. Makes bed with comforter.
5. Shares toys with friends.
6. Practices courtesy and manners with greetings, saying "please" and "thank you."
7. Uses tissue to blow nose.
8. Plays without constant supervision.
9. Toilets privately.

Four Year Olds
1. Helps put groceries away.
2. Follows a schedule for feeding pets.
3. Helps with simple yard work like picking up sticks and watering flowers.
4. Sweeps the floor.
5. Spreads butter on bread.
6. Prepares cold cereal for breakfast.
7. Gets the mail and newspaper.
8. Can play outside independently in a safe environment.
9. Helps unload the dishwasher.
10. Folds towels and helps put clothes away.
11. Chooses outfits and dresses self.
12. Bathes independently.
13. Takes bedding off of bed and takes to laundry for washing.
14. Wakes up with alarm clock.

Five Year Olds
1. Makes own sandwich and simple breakfast and cleans up.
2. Pours own drink.
3. Tears lettuce for salad.
4. Puts ingredients into a recipe.
5. Makes bed and cleans room.
6. Takes out the trash.
7. Has an allowance.
8. Feeds pets and cleans up after them.
9. Answers the phone.
10. Straightens bathroom after bathing.
11. Sorts laundry.
12. Vacuums the carpet.
13. Sets dinner table.
14. Ties shoes.

Six Year Olds
1. Cleans mirrors and windows, bathroom sink and tub.
2. Folds and hangs clean clothes and puts them away.
3. Helps clean out the car.
4. Writes thank you notes with assistance.
5. Straightens closet and drawers with assistance.
6. Helps with meal planning and grocery shopping.
7. Assists with cleaning garage.
8. Cares for bike and stores properly.
9. Assists with carrying in groceries.
10. Helps wash car.
11. Helps wash dog.

Seven Year Olds
1. Takes phone messages and writes them down.
2. Sweeps patio area.
3. Waters lawn and flowers.
4. Washes dog.
5. Writes thank you notes independently.
6. Sweeps and mops floor.
7. Assists with yard clean-up.
8. Dusts furniture.

Eight Year Olds
1. Runs own bath water or shower.
2. Straightens own closet and drawers.
3. Shops for and selects own clothing and shoes with parents using a budget.
4. Assist with cooking simple recipes.
5. Cuts flowers and makes centerpiece.
6. Assists with painting shelves or fence.
7. Feeds the baby.
8. Polishes silver, copper or brass items.
9. Assists with planting of flowers or vegetables.

Nine Year Olds
1. Changes sheets on bed and washes dirty sheets.
2. Operates washer and dryer.
3. Plans own birthday celebration.
4. Can independently clean and bandage a simple cut or scratch.
5. Arrives home from friend's house on agreed upon time.
6. Rakes yard and bags leaves.
7. Cooks simple recipe unassisted.

Ten Year Olds
1. Cleans refrigerator.
2. Prepares simple family meal.
3. Plants flowers unassisted.
4. Anticipates needs of others and offers to assist with their needs.
5. Shows interest in larger community by reading or watching current news.
6. Washes his or her own clothes.

Eleven Year Olds
1. Sets a formal table.
2. Cleans oven.
3. Mows the lawn.
4. Cleans pool and pool area.
5. Watches younger sibling while parent is otherwise engaged in house.
6. Puts younger sibling to bed.
7. Washes car without assistance.

Establishing A Morning Routine for Preschoolers

Many parents find getting to work on time to be a daily challenge thanks to their children. While the parent truly wants to be punctual, he is handicapped by a child who either does not want to get dressed independently or a child who seems to purposely move as slowly as possible. What is really going on is that the child has discovered that when she does not dress herself, she can count on her parents to do it for her. She is excused from responsible and cooperative behavior because her parents don't have the time to let the child dress, or they mistakenly think their child is not able to dress herself.

Children as young as two can dress themselves provided the clothing is not complicated. By age three a child should be dressing herself completely independently. If your child is not, don't despair. Meet with your child in the evening and explain the following, "Honey, you know how sometimes Mom and I get you dressed, or help you get dressed? Well, we realize it is not a help to you. We are treating you like a baby and you are certainly not a baby anymore! Starting tomorrow when we wake up, we'll let you take care of getting dressed and then having breakfast. We have to leave the house at 8:15. That's when the big hand is on the 3 and the little hand is on the 8. I'm sure you'll be ready but if you aren't, you can finish getting dressed at school."

Make sure you have alerted your child's preschool teacher that your child may arrive in her pajamas or partially dressed in the morning. The teacher can simply have your child go into the bathroom with her clothes and join the class when she is dressed. Be prepared to follow through with action. On the first morning that your child does not get ready in time, take her and her clothes to the car and drive to school. If she has not eaten, don't worry about it. A missed breakfast will not harm your child. She may cry and scream or yell. Be prepared to ignore it. Take her into her class and to her teacher who can take over from there.

It has been our experience that children rarely have to go to school without completely dressing more than three times. In most cases it only takes one time. Once the child realizes that she is no longer able to get Mom and Dad to provide special services or fight with her, she gives up the misbehavior.

Setting Up A Successful School Day Morning Routine

Sending your child off to school in the morning can be made much more pleasant by establishing a routine. The frantic search for a school bag or jacket can create an unpleasant start for child and parent. As a parent, you are in the strong position of being able to teach your child organizational techniques that help him depart the house for school prepared and on time.

Meet with your child prior to the first day of school to set up the school day morning routine. By involving your child in the decision making process you are letting your child know that his suggestions are valued. You also sidestep a potential power struggle since your child has input into planning his own schedule. Discuss and establish a place for storing coats, school book bags and lunch boxes. A panicked hunt for a lunch box in the morning can be avoided if everyone knows where to put their school items upon arriving home from school. Suggest to your child that he select his clothes for the next day and set them out the night before. Explain that you are available to help your child with his clothing selection if he would like, but that you will only offer help if your child would like your ideas.

Establish an appropriate time for your child to wake up in the morning. During the meeting show him how to use an alarm clock. Let your child know what time he will need to depart the house to meet the bus or get a ride to school. Discuss with your child how much time he might need to prepare for school in the morning. Give your child a time for setting the alarm that allows him enough time in the morning to wash, dress, eat and brush teeth before departing the house.

At the end of the meeting say to your child that you would like to meet after the first three days of school to hear how he thinks the routine that the two of you have set up is working. By inviting your child to set up his school morning routine you are letting your child know that you have confidence in your child's judgment and his ability to schedule his time wisely.

The Family Meal

The family meal serves as the foundation for a family's goodwill. Increasingly, parents miss this natural opportunity for deliberate encouragement. From preparing the meal to cleaning up afterwards, there are numerous ways to connect with your child positively.

Assisting a parent with dinner preparation is a task that affords children a chance to develop responsibility and to connect positively with their parent. Even a three year old can help tear lettuce to make the salad. It is a chance for a one-on-one conversation between parent and child as the two of them prepare the family meal. Setting the table is a contribution to the family meal with which another child can help.

Conversation at the family table helps to connect each member of the family to one another. Parents can use the family meal to encourage give and take conversations that demonstrate genuine interest in what each member of the family has to say. This is also an opportunity to extend children's interests away from themselves to things that happen in the larger society. Simple open-ended questions allow children and parents to share ideas and thoughts. For example, "I had lunch with a friend today. What did you do for lunch today?" Care must be taken to allow each member of the family to share in talk around the table. If one child is monopolizing the conversation, a parent can interject to give other children the chance to share their ideas. For example, "John, it was interesting to hear about the science experiment you and your class performed. Maggie, what science experiments has your class done this year?" This helps children learn that they each are valued members of the family and you can connect them to one other.

Table manners can be taught through deliberate encouragement. Rather than noticing who did not place napkins on laps, thank the people who did. Parents can also use the family meal to model good table manners. For instance, if a child asks a question and you have a mouthful of food, raise a finger and say after swallowing, "Sorry, I didn't want to speak with my mouth full."

Clean-up is a cooperative effort for those who did not cook. As plates are cleared and dishes are done, conversation and light banter can continue between family members. Children as young as three can assist with clearing the table. Recognize how children are contributing to clean up and avoid noticing who is not helping. You might say, "Thanks John for taking the placemats off of the table. You can put them here for someone to wash."

The family meal serves to unify the family and lets each person know he or she is a valued member of the family.

The User Friendly Kid's Bedroom

A clean and orderly child's bedroom is of great importance to many parents and of far less importance to most children. Achieving a clean and orderly bedroom is much simpler for the child who has a bedroom that is set up for her to clean easily. As you lay out your child's room, consider using the following guidelines to set her up for success.

Beds with comforters are easier for small hands to make on their own. Bedspreads require a lot more work. Children can pull a comforter up on a bed and put their pillows on it. A bedspread requires smoothing and tucking of pillows.

Choose open shelves for storage of toys rather than a toy box. A toy box invites mixing up and piling on of toys that result in a child having to pull everything out to get to the toy he wants to use. Toy boxes are also more likely to result in a toy being broken because other toys were piled on top of it. Open shelves not only make clean up easier, but they also promote care of toys.

Small toys, like animal sets and small manipulative sets, are best stored in individual containers on open shelves. You may wish to put a picture of the toy on the container so your child knows which toys belong in the container. This makes clean up and care of toys simpler for your child.

Consider how many toys your child owns. Limit the number of containers on the shelves and store extra toy containers in the closet. This gives you the opportunity to rotate toys so that your child continues to enjoy a variety of toys. This also invites her to clean up the toys in one container to exchange them for a container in the closet. You will also want to consider how many toys your child owns. While toys are necessary and important for children, it possible that you are over-buying if child has a challenge finding places to store toys when they are not in use.

A clothesbasket is a wonderful clothes hamper for your child. She can easily place her dirty clothes in it for washing. On laundry day she can help by bringing the clothesbasket to the laundry room. As your child gets older, a traditional clothes hamper can be used; but when purchasing it, bear in mind that it is your child, not you, who will be using it.

Establish the rule that food and drinks are to be eaten at a table. Spills are a challenge for anyone to clean up, let alone a child. By having a "no food" rule for bedrooms you avoid the problem altogether.

By setting up your child's room in a user-friendly manner, you help make cleaning of her room a simple task for her.

Feeding Baby

Just as the family meal is crucial to instilling a sense of connection among family members, so is the feeding of an infant. It is important for parents to establish a feeding schedule and routine with their infant. When an infant arrives, begin work on setting up a feeding schedule. Record feeding times so that you know when your child needs to eat. When it is time to feed your child, find a comfortable chair and put on some soft music. Give yourself a break by pouring a glass of water or a soft drink and propping up your feet. Speak and coo softly to your child while feeding him. Let the feeding time be a calm and relaxing exchange between you and your child.

If you have another child, invite the other child to sit near you. Sing or talk softly with the older child as your feed the baby so the older child feels included. Invite the older child to coo or sing softly with you. If you know your older child is restless later in the day when a feeding time is scheduled, arrange for her to watch a video or play with toys independently of you. This is one of the rare times when watching a children's program on television might be a help. Infant feeding time is an important time for parent and child to establish a bond. By setting up a warm and nurturing feeding time, you create a positive experience for your infant. When you invite older children to join you for this moment you help to connect siblings to one another.

The Family Road Trip

Traveling with children in the age of car seats and seatbelts can be a challenge. Unlike the days of old, small children are confined to a seat for the duration of the trip, which can lead to a less than pleasurable start to a vacation. While handheld games are nice, they are not always affordable. Consider a goody bag of inexpensive items to pass the time in the car. Coloring books, pads of paper, and crayons are handy items for car travel. Sticker books and puzzle games are inexpensive and fun. Purchase the items before the trip and keep them hidden. While traveling, give them out one at a time when your children get restless. The age-old alphabet game is great for children who can read. Look for a word on a sign beginning with A, then one with B and so on until the alphabet is complete. The first person to Z wins.

Should a squabble occur between two children, say, "I understand the two of you are angry with one another. Would you be willing to stop the argument for now since all of us are in the car?" If your children refuse, say nothing. If the argument continues, pull safely to the side of the road and stop. Again, do not speak. If the children ask why you are stopping say, "It is not safe to drive when the car is so loud. When you are finished, we will start driving again. It will take us longer to get where we are going, but we will be safe."

Instead of rest stops, do active stops. Select a restaurant with a playground and have the children play while you eat. When Mom and Dad are finished eating, get the children's food to go and let them eat it in the car. Choose rest areas and gas stations with grassy areas for your children to run around in before getting back into the car. With a little forethought, traveling by car can be a pleasant experience rather than a frazzling one.

A Tisket, A Tasket, The Family Laundry Basket

The family laundry is a big task that everyone contributes to creating. It also is a task that every family member needs to share in completing. Children can wash their own clothes by the age of ten. The groundwork for the chore of washing clothes can begin to be laid at the age of three.

At age three, provide your child with a clothes basket for his dirty clothes. On laundry day, ask your child to bring his clothesbasket to the washing machine. By the age of four your child can assist with folding towels. At the age of five invite your child to help you separate whites and darks. A nice way to teach your child why clothes are separated is to ask him what happens when red paint is mixed with white paint. Explain to him that the same thing can happen to clothes if they are mixed. By age six, a child can help hang clothes on a hanger and put them in his closet.

By the age of ten your child is ready to learn to do his laundry by himself. If he has not been assisting with the laundry tasks above, teach him in steps. When it comes to operating the washing machine, teach your child by letting him complete the task with your guidance. Show him how much laundry can fit into a load, then empty the washer and let him put his load of wash into the machine. Have him read the dials on the washing machine, then explain what each dial tells the washer to do. Provide an easy use cup for measuring the laundry detergent. Let your child measure out and pour in the detergent. Have him close the washer and let him set the water temperature. Once he has turned on the washer, explain to him that a load of wash will take about 25 minutes. Have him look at the clock to see when he will need to come back to put the laundry into the dryer. Do the same when it is time for him to start the dryer. Explain to him that clothes that are freshly dried are easier to fold and hang than clothes that have sat in the dryer and become wrinkled.

Be on hand for guidance the first several times that your child does his laundry on his own. This does not mean that you will do his laundry, but that you are in close proximity to answer questions he may have. Once he has completed his laundry for the first time, explain to your child that you do your laundry once a week. Ask him what day he would like to do his laundry so that you will be certain not to interfere with his wash day. Weekends are the most logical time for your child to complete his laundry. Having taught your child how to do his laundry, avoid the urge to save your child from the consequences of not doing his laundry. The most you might say the night before is, "I did my laundry so the washer is clear for you."   If your child does not wash his clothes, he will discover the natural consequence of having to wear some of his less favorite clothes until he does his laundry.

Be sure to acknowledge what a tremendous help it is to the family that your child can do his laundry.

Modeling Mistakes

Fear of making mistakes can prevent people from trying new things. It impedes a child from developing new skills and can affect a child's creativity. Parents are in a strong position to teach children how to handle their mistakes.

Children can look at their parents as being all-powerful and perfect. It is important for children to see that adults make mistakes and still move forward. Opportunities to model how to correct a mistake occur naturally in the household. Use these moments to instruct your child on how to move from a mistake to a solution. For example, Mom spills a glass of milk while pouring it. She can say, "I see I need to get some paper towels. I guess next time I'll hold the glass while I pour myself some milk." The tone for addressing mistakes is set by parents. By focusing on how to solve the problem rather than on the mistake, a parent provides her children with a template for forward movement rather than failure.

Look for opportunities to teach problem solving. If your child is building a block tower and is frustrated by the blocks falling, ask her what she could do to make the tower stronger. Invite your child to look for a solution rather than to dwell on the failure. Part of learning is making mistakes. When we model mistakes and how to correct mistakes in a non-judgmental way, we help children sidestep the discouragement of failure and replace it with the courage to solve problems.

The New Baby

The arrival of a baby is a big moment in any family. Prior to the baby's arrival parents are excited and share their excitement with the other children in the family. Many conversations occur between parents and children about how the children will be a big brother or big sister. Parents focus on how the "big" children will be able to help their new sibling. When the baby arrives, he sleeps a lot and is not much competition to a big brother or big sister. Parents focus their attention on the children who are now "big helpers." Initially the new baby's arrival starts out very well.

Several months later many parents report the start of jealously toward the baby on the part of their older children. It often coincides with the baby's development. The new arrival begins to sit up or crawl and the older children can feel threatened by the new child. Parents can avoid these problems by deliberately encouraging the older children.

Set up a play time with the older children before attending to the infant's needs. Invite the older children to assist with the infant's needs where possible. Have one parent interact with the older child while the other parent is involved with the infant. As the infant works on mastering new skills, share stories with the older children about the stages of development they mastered as babies. This helps connect the siblings to one another in a positive way. Should an older child exhibit jealousy toward the baby, minimize your response. Do not allow your child to gain your attention for misbehavior or you run the risk of the child using his jealousy to get you to focus on him.

Allowances

Establishing an allowance for your child gives her the opportunity to learn about money and responsible spending. A child is ready for an allowance at age five.

As you set up the allowance, meet with your child to outline what an allowance might be used to purchase. An allowance for a young child is used for non-basic items such as a toy, snack, or family gift. The parent decides the amount of the allowance. As you meet with your child you might say, "I know that there are times when we are out that you would like to buy something for yourself or another person. As a part of our family you need some money to spend. An allowance will provide you with money for things that you might want to buy from time to time. Your allowance is your money and you get to decide how it will be spent." Let the child know the amount of the allowance and when the allowance will be paid.

As you set up an allowance with your child it is important to avoid tying an allowance in to completion of chores or duties. The allowance is not a reward or payment for jobs completed. Family chores are performed because they help the family, not because a child is paid for them. This does not mean that there are not tasks which a parent might pay a child to complete. The tasks that we pay children to perform would fall outside of the routine chores that each family member helps to complete for the benefit of the family. The allowance provides your child with money she can use if she wishes to purchase something herself. The allowance for a young child is not large.

Once the allowance has been started, you will have the opportunity to begin teaching your child spending habits. She may say, "I am going to use this to buy a toy." Do not be surprised if when you and she are out shopping, she decides to use the money for a snack. Let her make her purchase. If the topic of the toy comes up again, you can ask, "What would happen if you put half of your allowance in your bank each week?" By letting your child decide how she will use the money, she learns how to monitor her spending. You may find that your child asks for an advance on her allowance. In a friendly tone say, "I understand that you wish you had some money right now, you will be paid your allowance on allowance day." Part of money management is learning that once the money is spent, your child will not have any money until allowance day.

At some point, your child may attempt to compare her allowance with another family's allowance. Avoid engaging in an explanation of why you do not pay the same allowance. A simple response is all that is needed. For example, "Each family is different. This is what our family does."

As your child gets older, you will want to increase the amount of the allowance. You will also want to turn over the cost of more items to your child. Turn over the costs of items to a child gradually. When going to a movie with your child explain that you will cover the cost of the ticket and she can cover the cost of any food she wants to buy. A child who wishes to go to the movies with her friends can reasonably be expected to pay for that out of her own funds. By gradually increasing the amount of the allowance and the payment responsibility, you encourage your child's money management skills.

School Performance

Once your child begins school, parents need to have a plan for discussions regarding a child's progress. School is a child's responsibility. Your child's performance in school is information that his teacher will share with your child and with you. Unfortunately without a plan for discussion of report cards, it can easily become a battleground among siblings with a child's school performance becoming the casualty. School performance is not a competition.

At the end of a grading period, set aside a time to meet with your child so he can discuss his report card with you. Choose a time when you are alone with your child. If you have more than one child, meet with each child individually and privately. Siblings may choose to discuss their report cards with one another, but do not allow yourself to discuss one child's school performance in front of the other child.

As you meet with your child, allow him to tell you about the grades he has earned. On subjects in which your child has performed well you might say, "I see that you have done well in math. What do you like about the math you have been learning?" This provides your child with a chance to share his accomplishments with you. You are deliberately encouraging your child. Avoid rewards for good school performance. School is a child's responsibility. When we reward a child for his performance we send the mistaken message that he should be paid to perform. Rewards are a form of bribery and they steal from the child the opportunity to take personal pleasure in his accomplishments.

At some point your child may perform poorly in a subject. After your child has shared his grade with you, you might say, "What do you think you can do to improve your grade?" Listen to his solution. If his solution is a sound one, convey your agreement with his plan. If his solution is not a sound one, say, "I have some ideas that might help you improve your grade." Then share your ideas. You may also need to set up a system for monitoring your child's progress in a problem area. Care must be taken as you do this. If you become the school work police, your child can resist your well intentioned, but overly controlling efforts. When this occurs, your child is at risk of continuing to perform poorly. This can occur because the issue for the child is no longer school performance, but rather it becomes demonstrating to you that you will not control him.

Keep in mind that when you take action designed to improve behavior or achievement, it is wise to observe the influence of the action. Remember that there is a purpose or use to behavior and that no one is willing to stand in a position of inferiority. Occasionally you may find that you have applied a technique that your child perceives as relegating him to an inferior position and your child may decide to compensate by defying or punishing you. When this occurs, it is wise to ask your child if he thinks the remedy is unfair or if it feels like punishment. If this is the child's perception, then invite him to help modify the technique. This is an excellent way to side step power struggles.

Avoid punitive measures as a solution to poor grades. Taking away a child's electronic game is not going to result in your child obtaining a better grade. The child does not use the game while he is in school. Offering to quiz your child before a test is a concrete solution that can help. It is proactive rather than punitive. Helping your child to establish good study habits is also a concrete solution. You can help your child set up a time once a week for him to review the material his class has learned in the past week. Offer to be available for the review, but ultimately, the review is the child's responsibility.

In some rare cases, it can be that a child has so many demands on his time, that good study habits are prevented by extracurricular activities. While playing recreation league sports, taking dance lessons, participating in scouting are important, they are not the work of the child. If this is occurring you can say, "I realize that you do not have the time you need to complete your job. That can happen to me sometimes. When that happens, I have to bring work home to finish and that means that I have less time for me. I know that you enjoy playing ball, but you need more time for your school work. I will call your coach and explain that you will be able to practice once a week, but not three times a week. This will give you two more nights a week for your school work. I know you will be working on improving your grade. Let's meet back at the end of next week and you can let me know how it is working for you."

At the end of the week, meet with your child so he can share how the week has gone. If he has made progress, give him the choice of resuming the three practices, or continuing with once a week. If he chooses to resume the three-day a-week practices explain that while you are confident he is able to manage his studies and activities, should he have more problems, the extracurricular activity would have to be stopped. If he has not made progress, continue with the altered schedule. This places the responsibility for improved school work with your child.

Chores

Helping out with chores at home is an excellent way to instill responsibility in small children. One of the troublesome aspects of chores is that children may choose not to do them. In many cases, parents then nag children or try to force them to complete their chores. As a way of avoiding such a power struggle, try making a job chart. The chart will list all the jobs that need to be done in the course of a week as well as some monthly jobs. Beside the names of the jobs is a blank chart. The jobs are not assigned to anyone. Rather, when a household member completes a task, she puts her initials in the space beside the job name. This lets other people know that the job was completed that day as well as who is lending a hand around the house.

The beauty of this job chart is that it encourages participation in chores. In a traditional home when children do not complete chores a parent nags them until they are done. Children end up in power struggles with parents over household chores or they whine and drag their feet over chores until they manage to get a parent to "assist" them with their chores. Using the job chart above, parents are placing the emphasis on the contributions made to the family by their children.

Children want to be recognized for their contributions to the family. When they initial the chart, make a point of thanking them for the tasks they have completed. Say nothing to the child who is not doing any chores. The visual job chart and your verbal recognition of the children who are helping out will encourage the resistant child to lend a hand. She wants to count for something in the family. Let her discover on her own that she can count as a helper in the family.

If she continues to refuse to complete chores, let logical consequences occur. When she wants you to play a game with her, explain, "Honey, I would love to play with you, but there are a lot of chores that haven't been done. I will have to complete those before I can play. If you would like, you may help with some of them. That might make it possible for us to play later." If the child completes chores, do your best to spend play time with her. If she chooses not to, then you are unavailable. Stick to your position. Let her discover that she can choose not to cooperate but that cooperation is a two-way street. You can choose not to cooperate as well. Once you have made your first statement, go about your business and let her make her choice.

Sample Job Chart

Chore	Sun	Mon	Tue	Wed	Thur	Fri	Sat
Make bed							
Set table							
Cook dinner							
Wash dishes							
Sweep floor							
Vacuum							
Mop kitchen							
Dust furniture							
Clean bathroom							
Wash clothes							
Put away wash							
Grocery shopping							
Put groceries up							
Take out trash							
Put away dishes							
Clean room							
Straighten den							
Get mail & paper							
Mow or rake yard							

Extracurricular Activities

Children can benefit from participating in group activities for sports, drama, music, scouting, dance and other enrichment activities. The challenge for parents and children is to ensure that the activity is one that is enriching rather than a chore for either the parent or the child, or both. Parents must consider what is realistic given their time constraints and their child's time constraints. A child's genuine interest in the activity must also be considered.

Parents can make children aware of the various extracurricular activities that they can facilitate with their child. Parents must also set the ground rules for how many activities are possible. Rushing from soccer to dance three times a week with a child can create a problem for the family. Additional lessons are meant to be enjoyable learning experiences for a child and provide pleasant spectator moments for parents. Parents must take care not to over schedule their child, creating an unnecessary burden on the family unit.

Extracurricular activities are also opportunities for children to learn how to budget their time wisely. They are play activities that occur after their work is done. As children move into elementary school and have responsibilities like homework, parents will want to have a friendly discussion with their child regarding time management. Set up the simple guideline that baseball practice comes after homework is complete.

Sometimes a child can begin a sport or music lesson only to discover that he does not like the activity. If this occurs, parents should meet with their child to discuss what the child dislikes about the activity. If the child finds the activity discouraging, ask the child what he dislikes about the activity and whether he would like to discontinue it or would like to try it for a little longer to see if he likes it any better. Extracurricular activities are meant to enhance a child's experiences, not to discourage him.

The Birds and the Bees Talk

The sexual education of a child can send parents running to the bookstore in terror. As a parent, if you find yourself dreading this important discussion with your child, it might help you to think back on what you would have done differently when your parents spoke with you about the topic. Many parents struggle with this discussion. Shying away from the discussion, or leaving it to your child to learn at school fails to provide your child with a trusted person to turn to when questions regarding human sexuality arise during her late childhood and adolescence.

The age at which a child is ready for a discussion about human sexuality can vary. A good rule of thumb is to check with your child's elementary school to learn when they will teach the unit on introduction to human sexuality. Many schools do this as part of their fourth grade health curriculum. Naturally, at the age of 10 your child is not ready to learn all aspects of human sexuality. However, it is important for parents to be one of their child's educators on this subject. It is also important for parents to realize that there will not be one definitive discussion about sex with their child. Your child will continue to need guidance and have questions about this topic throughout childhood and adolescence. By initiating the conversation you are establishing yourself as an invaluable resource for your child over the next several years.

Set aside a time for you and your child to have this discussion. Open the discussion by explaining to your child that she is getting older. Over the next few years her body will begin changing and developing. Ask your child if she knows what sexual education or the birds and bees means. It is possible your child might blush and stammer "Yes." Explain to your child that you thought she might have some questions and that you would like to answer as many as you can. Ask your child if she would be okay with having such a discussion. The next step is to determine what your child knows. Say, "It would be a help to me to know what you have heard so far. That way I won't go over things that you may already know."

By opening the door for your child to share with you what she knows, you put the discussion at your child's level and can avoid covering more than your child wants to know. Listen calmly and carefully to your child. Do not interrupt and do not question your child. What she is doing takes tremendous courage on her part. Most children mistakenly believe talking about sex is taboo. This is a myth that you are working to dissolve during your discussion. Once your child has stopped, offer your information. Your child's response will serve as your guide for what to address. Some of what she says may be mistaken. Some of what she says will be correct. Do not be surprised if she knows far more than you had expected. That is not uncommon.

After you have finished giving your information, ask your child if she has any questions. She may have a few or she may have many. Answer them all, even if the answer is, "I actually don't know, but I will find out for you." This helps establish you as a resource person to come to when your child has questions in the future.

Visiting Friends and Relatives

Parenting a child in view of family and friends calls for confidence and perseverance on the part of the parent. Your child rearing approaches will not necessarily be the same as those of your friends and family. It takes courage on the part of a parent to ignore real or imagined criticism from others. Here are a couple of guidelines to keep in mind when visiting friends and relatives.

Maintain your child's schedule and bedtime routines as much as possible. While your brother may feel that bedtime is "whenever" during family gatherings, you know better. As a caring parent who wants his child to enjoy all of the family visit, be prepared to ignore comments when you put your child down for evening at his regular bedtime. The next day will be far more pleasant for you and your child if your child is well rested.

Set aside some quiet time each day with your young child. Use this calm time to allow your child to interact with you independently of the larger family group. In a room of ten people, you and your child naturally will not interact as you normally would at home. While this is part of the fun of a friends or family gathering, it can lead to attention seeking behavior on the part of young children if they are not provided some time away with their parent in the smaller family unit. Take a quiet walk with your child to ask him how he is enjoying his visit. Ask your child what he has learned about the people he has been visiting. Your one-on-one time encourages your child to continue to enjoy the larger gathering while also enjoying his connection to his immediate family.

Recognize that your parenting approach may not be in agreement with what another parent is doing. While another parent may excuse his child from helping with dinner clean-up, do not respond to complaints from your children such as "Why do we have to do the dishes, our cousins don't!" Parenting of children is not a job that is turned off and on based upon the situation. Set yourself up to enjoy visits with family and friends for the present and the future.

Reading Aloud With a Child

Reading aloud with children has so many benefits. It is an excellent form of deliberate encouragement. Reading with children encourages their interest in reading. The establishment of a bedtime reading ritual is one that parents will want to begin with the children before age two. Simple stories fast become favorites to your child. She may request the same story again and again. This is to be expected. Also to be expected is that your child will begin to join you in the reading of a favorite story as she memorizes it. This is a sign that your child is growing to love books and reading. When reading to a child, ask the child what she thinks will happen next in the story. This helps your child to develop her story comprehension skills.

The nightly reading of stories should not stop when your child begins to read. As your child grows older, select books that are more complex and which can be read over several nights. Invite your child to suggest books for reading. Children enjoy being read to aloud throughout their elementary school years. This special time between parent and child provides your child with a clear message that you and she can enjoy one another's company. The message is simple. "I like spending this time with you."

As your child grows older you can pave the way for book discussions. Ask your child for suggestions of a good book to read on your own. After you have read it, have an informal discussion about the book with your child. You are indicating to your child that you value her suggestions. You have also created a common interest which you and your child can enjoy conversing about together.

Hello! I'm Happy To See You!

The evening pick-up routine between a child and parent at the child development center is a very special time for a child. It is the opportunity for a parent to encourage a child by asking the child about his day.   It is also a time for the parent to share with the child what the parent did during the day. Children are happy to see their parent and naturally want to talk with them and reconnect with them. It is reasonable for children to want their parent's undivided attention from the moment a parent arrives at the classroom until the parent and children arrive home. Unfortunately, cell phones can intrude upon this child-parent time. When a parents answer a call during the pick-up time, they mistakenly place more importance on the call than on their relationship with their child. Parents can stop this intrusion upon the child/parent connection by choosing not to answer their phone.

Greet your child with a smile and an open-ended question that invites a longer response from your child. For instance, "I saw you playing with the puzzles. What pictures were in the puzzle?" Questions like, "What did you do today?" often result in the vague response, "I played." By asking a question linked to something you observed your child doing, you give your child a context for a conversation. If the classroom has a lesson plan posted, take a look at it. This can make it possible for you to ask questions directly related to what your child did during the day.

If you are picking up two children, pick up the older child first. The older child can assist with holding the door as you go into the room of the younger child. You can use the conversation started with the older child as a connection builder with the younger child. For example, "Hello Jeremy! Mia was working on a puzzle just now. I see you are play cooking. What are you cooking?"

Give and take conversations between child and adult at pick-up time are important opportunities for encouraging children and letting children know they are valued.

The Family Outing

Family outings can be enjoyable or disastrous. Their success lies in good planning and information sharing. Prior to the day's event, meet with your children to give them information that will help them know what to expect.

Share with your children where the family will be going. Be sure to explain when you will leave the house, how long you and your children will be at the destination and when you will come back home. Do this in terms they can understand. For instance, "We are going to the zoo. We will leave in the morning after breakfast and come home about the time you get up from nap each day."

Let your children know what activities your family will do together while they are at the destination. Ask your children what rules everyone will need to follow while they are on the outing. Establish with your children what will happen if the outing is not going well. For instance, "I don't think this will happen, but if there is a problem, we will need to stop and meet to discuss a solution. If we cannot agree on a solution, we will leave and try visiting at another time." Discuss what allowable costs will occur. If a trip to a gift shop is planned, set up the cost guidelines ahead of time. If lunch will be eaten out, discuss what meal is within the price range you can afford.

By sharing information and necessary guidelines, you set yourself and your children up for a pleasant family event.

Board Games With The Family

A great way to deliberately encourage children is to play board games. Board games give children and parents an opportunity to connect with each other for no other purpose than to have fun. At the same time, they teach children turn taking, how to follow directions and how to handle winning and losing. Simple games like Memory, Candyland and Hi-Ho Cherrio are best with young children. As your child grows older more complex games can be played. Card games like Go Fish, Old Maid, UNO, and Concentration also can provide a special family fun night.

A mistake that parents can make when playing games with children is to let them win. This is not only discouraging to a child, but it is also disrespectful. Part of playing a game is to learn how to play better. When parents allow children to win, they mistakenly send a message that they do not believe their child is capable of learning how to play a game. It also mistakenly teaches children that they should win every game they play.

Challenges may arise if a child becomes angry about playing a game poorly. This provides a natural opportunity for parents to let a child discover that losing is part of the game. If a child is upset about playing a game poorly, say, "Sometimes we lose when we play games and sometimes we win. What I really like is playing the game so we can laugh and have fun together. If the game is not fun for someone, they are welcome to stop playing. Would you like to stop playing?" Give your child the chance to leave the game if she wishes. If your child decides to continue playing but chooses also to continue to get angry then you might say in a friendly but firm voice, "I see that the game is not going to be so much fun tonight. I am going to stop playing for tonight." Without any further words, put up your playing pieces and exit the game. It is likely your children will ask you to stay. They may even become angry with the child who was misbehaving during the game. Do not re-enter the game. Let your actions speak for you. By letting children discover that the purpose of game night is to have fun, you ensure that you and your children will have many enjoyable game nights in the future.

Notes of Encouragement

From time to time your child will struggle to master some skill, or behavior. A note of encouragement is an excellent method for recognizing the contributions your child is making for himself or for others. A simple hand-written note placed in a lunch box can provide your child with the confidence that he can meet the challenges that face him.

Care must be taken in the wording of the letter. The focus of your message should be on the actions of the child rather than on how you feel about what he has done. For example, suppose your child shared with you that he befriended a new child at school who was lonely. This is an excellent opportunity for written encouragement. You might write, "Thank you for sharing how you helped Jenna to find a friend at school. Your kindness helped make her first day at school much happier."

A child who masters riding a bike after several falls might be written the following note. "You showed a lot of courage learning how to ride your bike. You didn't let a few falls stop you. I know you will enjoy riding your bike with your friends."

While you do not want to overuse written encouragement, it is certainly a valid tool for communicating to your child that he is capable of solving problems and challenges. It sends the message that you believe your child has what is called for in life.

A Day for Just Me and You

In families with more than one child, it can be very encouraging to plan an outing with one child. This is particularly important if you find that one of your children is engaging in misbehavior, which is usually a warning sign that your child is discouraged. Set aside an hour for a trip to the library followed by lunch. Take an hour to fly kites or play ball with your child at the local park. The purpose of the outing is simple. You are connecting with your child for a friendly get together. The message that is sent to the child is invaluable. The discouraged child senses that she is okay, period. The outing is not linked to any behavior or accomplishment. It is just a time to have your undivided attention. The message that is sent is simple: I love you and I like you.

Parents who work and have more than one child can find themselves struggling to manage to find time to get away with just one child. It can help to put the time into perspective. One hour a month with four children is only four hours. If you are a single parent, arrange with another single parent to help one another out by watching each other's children so that each of you can schedule this special child and parent activity. The one-on-one outing is a common early childhood memory for many adults. By setting aside this time with you and your child, you provide a message of encouragement that can last your child a lifetime.

Funny Family Stories

A deliberate encouragement technique for both children and parents is the telling of funny family stories. A wonderful part of any childhood is the humorous antics that a child performs. The stories about these incidents are of great interest to your child. They are also part of your family's history. While sitting around the dinner table, or while doing dishes together you can create a very special evening by sharing stories about silly events that occurred with your child.

Obviously, care must be taken not to share a story that is at the expense of a child, but if you think back on your child's early years, you will no doubt have a few come to mind. This form of humorous story telling serves to bond family members to one another. When sharing funny stories, you can also share some of the family stories from your own childhood. Children enjoy hearing about the antics of their parents as children. This helps connect your children to your family of origin. It is not unlike watching home videos, but because it takes place in the format of oral story telling, you are passing down the history of a family.

Do not be surprised at being asked to tell the stories again and again. Your children confirm their sense of connection and significance within the family when they hear the stories.

Bedtime for Baby

Bedtime is one of the first challenges faced by new parents. It is also where some of the first mistakes are made. Using the approach below you are better able to turn the bedtime challenge into a parenting success.

Once your baby has been fed and changed, and you have spent one-on-one time at play with her, it is time for nap. We suggest putting your baby in her crib and allowing your child to go to sleep independently of you. It is not uncommon for your baby to cry when you first place her in her crib for a nap. If you choose to pick your child up and rock or comfort her until she falls asleep, then you begin to teach her that she needs to have you "help" her go to sleep. It is far better to allow your child to cry herself to sleep. It is an act of love to allow your child to learn how to go to sleep independently of you. Establishing a nap and bedtime routine is one of the first tasks a new parent has. It takes courage and love on the part of new parents to let the baby discover that she can go to sleep all by herself.

If your child is still crying after 15-20 minutes, go into the room and silently rub the baby's arm or face. Resist the temptation to pick your child up and comfort her. She is sleepy and needs to rest. Be respectful of your baby and allow her to discover that she can handle nap time and bedtime all by herself. Keep in mind that before you put your child down for sleep, you had played with your child and met both her physical and social/emotional needs. Babies need sleep and down time to process the incoming stimulation they receive. By giving your child this down time you are aiding her development.

Bedtime Blues

Bedtime has been known to have even the calmest of parents pulling out their hair. If the bedtime routine in your house isn't working, we suggest using the technique below.

After reading a story to your child with him in his bed, give your child a hug and kiss good night. Then turn off his light and leave the room. Ignore requests or calls by your child to get you back into the room. If your child comes out of his room, ignore him and go about your business. If your child tries to join you, go to your room and lock the door. If he follows you and begins crying or pounding on the door, continue to ignore him. Your child is trying to get you to make one of two mistakes. Either he is trying to get you into the power struggle of "making" him go to bed, or he is trying to obtain special services by getting you to "comfort" him to sleep. In both cases, it is terribly important for the child to discover that going to bed is his responsibility, not yours.

Be prepared to go the distance. Children who have had 20 minute tantrums in the past when parents have tried to get them to bed will have to be waited out. Have a pair of earphones and a book ready for yourself. If the child falls asleep outside of your door after having a tantrum, quietly take your child and put him in his bed. Keep in mind that you are instilling independence in your child when you allow him to learn how to go to sleep by himself, and you are conveying confidence in his ability to handle the task.

Losing the Pacifier

Around the age of 9 to 12 months it is time for parents to take the pacifier away from the baby. This presents a bigger challenge for parents than for the infant. On making the decision to discard the pacifier, parents must agree to an all or nothing approach. The child is too young to get the pacifier by herself. Only an adult can retrieve the item for the baby.

When stopping the use of the pacifier, the parents simply get rid of the pacifiers. Be prepared for the baby to cry. Parents will need to stand their ground and not cave in to the baby's cries for the pacifier. To give in to the child's tears teaches the child that crying works when she wants something. There is no gradual way to take away a pacifier. The approach is final; the pacifier is history. Parents who are expecting another baby, will want to take the pacifier away from the older child several months before the new baby arrives. This reduces the likelihood the older child will associate the new baby with the pacifier and helps parents to avoid the older child taking the baby's pacifier.

Separation Anxiety

Many a child has discovered that hanging on to a parent and crying means that Mom or Dad stays longer in the morning. If this is how you leave your child each morning, the following suggestion will be of help to you.

Your child has discovered that if he cries and hangs onto your leg, he is rewarded by a longer goodbye in the morning. It is not pleasant for either one of you, but it has succeeded in getting you to play into your child's behavior goal. Rather than spend any more time trying to soothe your child or ease him into his day, focus your energies on teaching him self reliance. When you take your child into his room, give him a hug and a kiss. Tell him, "I'll see you tonight honey and you can tell me who you played with today." Then walk out the door. If your child has a tendency to cling to you, put him into the arms of his teacher to prevent him from stopping you.

Stand outside of the closed classroom door if you like. Typically, children stop crying 5 to 10 minutes after their parents leave. In many cases, it stops almost immediately. The reason for this is that the tears and clinging were meant for the parent. Once the usefulness of the misbehavior has been removed, the child finds other more productive things to do. On the other hand, if a child discovers that 5 minutes of tears gets Mom or Dad to stay longer in the morning, he will be prepared to go 10 minutes the next day. It takes love and firm resolve for parents to let their child discover that he cannot use "water power" with his parents. Parents who avoid the pitfalls of separation anxiety are encouraging independence and self reliance on the part of their child. Their child learns to solve problems on his own rather than expecting Mom or Dad to solve them for him.

Bye Bye Blanky

Many children develop an attachment to a blanket or a soft toy. While this is not uncommon, it can present problems for a child as she gets older. Parents can find themselves frantically searching through a diaper bag or room when a child discovers that the blanket or toy is not present. This is when a parent needs to intervene. While a child might like her blanket or toy, if the child becomes distressed when the item is not present, then the item has crossed over from being a source of enjoyment to one of dependence.

Should this happen, parents need to let their child discover that the presence of the blanket, while nice, is not necessary. The child has mistakenly drawn the conclusion that her security lies with the blanket or toy. The absence of the blanket or toy leads to tears and the well meaning, but mistaken parents retrieve the item to comfort the child. Parents need to avoid allowing a child to become so attached to an item that it causes distress by its absence. This will mean listening to tears and protests from a child. The most a parent might say is, "I know that you would like your blanket, but it is not here." The parent can go on about her day until the child decides to join her.

Caving in to a child's demands for a blanket or toy undermines the child's courage. It mistakenly sends the message that the child lacks the courage to go to child care or visit a friend without her item. While having a favorite blanket or soft toy is not uncommon, allowing the child to bring it with her everywhere can lead the child to mistakenly believe that she needs the item.

Toilet Training

Most children are ready for toilet training between the ages of 20 months and 27 months. The child does need to be verbal so he can tell you if he is wet and when he needs to use the bathroom. Once you decide to begin toilet training parents will want to use cloth training pants rather than disposable training pants. A very important part of toilet training is that the child feels the discomfort of wet or soiled pants. Disposable training pants prevent this from occurring.

Dress him in clothing he can easily get out of to reduce the chance of accidents taking place. Dresses are ideal for little girls. Elastic waistband pants are ideal for little boys. Overalls or clothing that snaps in the crotch is frustrating for small fingers. Remember, you want to dress the child for success. Next, have a brief conversation with your child about toilet training. Say, "Honey, now that you are getting to be such a big boy you won't need to wear diapers. You can wear big boy pants and use the potty all by yourself like Mom and Dad do. When you have to go, just let us know. Sometimes we'll ask you if you need to go. If you don't need to use the bathroom, just let us know."

Explain to your child that when he needs to use the bathroom, he can pull down his pants and stand in front of, or sit on the toilet. Invite him to show you how he can do that. When he does, you might say, "I see you understand what to do." Ask him if he would like to try to use the toilet. If he doesn't go to the bathroom, have him pull up his pants. You might say, "Boy, you sure did a nice job of pulling your pants up and down." Focus on the child's helpful behavior. Avoid commenting on the absence of urination. If the child does urinate, say, "Thank you for using the toilet honey! I know you enjoy doing things all by yourself!" Keep your comments focused on what the child did rather than what he did not do. Do not praise or reward his toileting successes. Praise and reward mistakenly teach children that they only need do things for payoffs. Encouragement, on the other hand, focuses on how the child's actions are a help to him personally.

Pleasantly ask the child to use the bathroom every hour. If he refuses to go when you offer him the chance, do not force him. Attempts to force a child to use the toilet or to remain on the toilet for long periods of time often result in the child deciding to fight us. Children who fight us over toilet training win every time because all they need do to defeat us is to soil their pants. Be respectful of the child. If he says he does not need to use the bathroom, accept it. If he has an accident, avoid the temptation to criticize or correct the child. Comments like "Next time you need to get to the bathroom sooner" are discouraging to the child and can result in a power struggle with the child.

Instead, try saying, "Sweetheart, I see you had an accident. You can take those pants off and put on some clean ones. When you get finished, come and join me." Make light of accidents but place the responsibility for cleaning up after the accident with the child.   One of the biggest mistakes made by parents is to offer advice and to change the child. It steals from the child the opportunity to learn how to solve the problem by himself.

After you have been toilet training for a while, you might want to invite your child to go shopping with you to pick out several pairs of underpants. Each day your child begins the day in the new underpants he chose. Pack his bag with the training pants. In the event of an accident, your child will have to change into the old, clunky training pants. However, if your child remains dry, he will be able to keep his "big boy pants" on. The "pretty panties" or "big boy pants" technique is useful for fine-tuning your child's toilet training after you have gotten the toilet training under way rather than at the beginning since accidents will take place more frequently at the onset of training.

Cleaning Up Toys

A very good way for parents to teach a child responsibility is by giving a child chores she can assist with at home. One of the first chores parents give their child is cleaning up her toys. Often this is where the first break down on completion of chores takes place. Dad tells his daughter to clean up her toys. Ten minutes later he comes into the room to find his child still at play with no headway made and one of two approaches occurs. In the case of a pampering parent, Dad will offer to "help" his daughter with toy clean-up. What really happens is that the child discovers she is excused from toy cleaning responsibility because she can count on Dad to bail her out. In the case of a coercive parent, Dad tries to force his child to clean up by threats or shouting. In both scenarios, the parent has failed to instill responsible behavior in his child.

The following technique can help parents teach children that they are responsible for cleaning up their toys. At a neutral time, meet with your child to say, "Honey, when it's time to clean up your toys Mom and Dad need your help. We will give you 15 minutes to clean up your toys. You will probably clean your toys up before that. When that happens, come and get us to show us how you helped. If for some reason, you decide not to clean up, then one of us will clean up your toys but we will put your toys up and you will not have them to play with for the rest of the day."

Having outlined your course of action, be prepared to follow through. The next time your child doesn't clean up her toys after 15 minutes, go into the room and put what she was playing with out of reach for the remainder of the day. Be prepared to act quickly and then leave the room to avoid making temper tantrums useful. Using a logical consequence for choosing not to clean up toys helps parents avoid the risk of the power struggle offered by the child who is looking to get Mom or Dad to "make" her clean up her toys. It also avoid pampering the child as she learns that choosing not to clean up her toys means the toys will not be available for her to use.

As a way of encouraging toy clean up for the future, make a point of letting your child show off her clean up job to you. After seeing it you might want to say, "Honey, you did that so fast! Would you like to read a story together before dinner?"

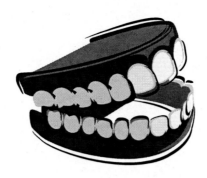

Biting

When toddlers and young children want their way it is not uncommon for them to try to accomplish this by biting. Many children try biting at some point in their early years. What determines whether the child continues to use biting as a means of getting his way is the reaction of the person who is bitten. Parents are in a strong position to stop biting. If your child bites you, stop what you are doing and say, "When you hurt me, I choose not to be with you." Then take action and walk to another room in the house. Biting can be an attempt to draw you into a power struggle. Let your child discover that if he chooses to bite, you will choose not to be around him. Stay clear of talking with a child about why he should not bite, instead let your actions speak for you. When the child has calmed down, return to the room. If the child bit you to get his way in some form of play, do not return to that type of play. Instead start another activity. Children understand delay of gratification at a very young age. If the child bit you because he wanted a toy the two of you were playing with, you will want to put the toy up on your way out of the room. When you return to the room, begin another activity or task.

Look for opportunities to encourage your child's socialization skills later in the day. If you and your child are playing with blocks, ask him to pass you a block. Then thank him for being a friend and sharing with you. This sends a loud and clear message that kind and cooperative behaviors are what you value.

If your child is biting at child care, refrain from talking with him about "not biting." When we discuss not engaging in a misbehavior we are still unwittingly providing attention to the child for the misbehavior. Instead, ask your child which friends he enjoyed playing with during the day. Connect with your child on what he is doing that is friendly rather than on those things that are unkind. This helps to teach caring behavior.

Bedwetting

Children who wet their bed usually do so for one of two reasons. In the first case, the child may be attempting to get unnecessary attention or service from Mom or Dad. By wetting the bed, the child is able to get Mom or Dad to change her clothes and put on fresh sheets. In the second case, the child may be trying to demonstrate to Mom and Dad that she will decide when she is going to go to the bathroom, not them. Regardless of what the parents do: cutting off liquids, taking the child to the bathroom several times before bed, etc., the child still wets the bed. The bedwetting is the child's way of saying "I am in charge of me."

In either case, the suggestion below can help parents avoid making bedwetting a useful form of misbehavior to the child. At a neutral time, sit down with your child and explain the following in a respectful and friendly way. "Honey, Dad and I have been acting as though you aren't able to keep your bed dry. We realize that's silly. You are a big girl and can keep your bed dry without our help. From now on, we will leave it up to you to decide whether you need to go to the bathroom. We think you'll do fine. If for some reason you should wet the bed, you can change your pajamas and the sheets on your bed. There are extra sheets in the hall closet so you can take the wet sheets off and put dry sheets on the bed. When we get home in the evening, you can take care of washing your dirty sheets while we are cooking dinner."

The above technique places the responsibility for keeping the bed dry with the child. In this way, parents avoid playing into the child's mistaken goal of behavior and instead encourage the child's independence. This technique has been used with children as young as three. Initially, the child may think it is pretty cool to strip her bed and put the sheets in the washing machine. However, the novelty soon wears off and the child comes to the realization that wetting the bed makes extra work for her. We suggest having the child wash her sheets during a time when she would normally be playing. This helps bring home to the child that the only person inconvenienced by the bedwetting is herself.

Fearfulness

Whether it is bees, roaches, thunderstorms, or the dark, many people have one or two unreasonable fears lurking in their minds. These fears are unpleasant and in some cases, embarrassing. Parents have a responsibility to avoid planting such fears in children's minds. Fear is a learned response and parents are children's most influential teachers.

If you have experience with an unreasonable fear, try thinking for a moment about the item that you do not like. Think carefully about how you feel when you are faced with that item. It's not a very nice feeling, is it? Now think about your child. Do you want your child to spend his lifetime feeling the way that you do about that item? If not, then curb your behavior the next time that you are faced with the item you fear. If you are afraid of bees let that be your own fear, not your child's. The next time a bee comes near, have the courage to say in a calm voice, "I see a bee nearby. I'm going to move away from it slowly." In this way, you teach your child how to solve a problem. Once you are out of your child's sight and earshot, feel free to indulge in your fearful behavior. Just don't teach your child your fears. Children often follow their parent's examples of fear. If they see that you are scared, they will assume there is good reason to be afraid and they will be fearful of the same item.

It takes courage on the part of a parent as well as love not to communicate fearfulness to a child. Keep in mind that children who have learned to be problem solvers also tend to have fewer fears because they live in a world that is under their control to a greater extent than does the dependent child.

Avoiding the Food Fight

As a toddler begins to take over the responsibility of feeding herself, it is not uncommon for the child to experiment with throwing food. There are several reasons why a child would decide to throw food. The child might be trying to get her parent to feed her thereby excusing the child from responsible behavior. The child might be trying to draw the parent into a power struggle in which the parent tries to stop the child from throwing the food. The child may also no longer be hungry. In all of the above situations, it is important for you to let your child discover that playing with food is not acceptable and that she cannot use such misbehavior to get you involved with her. Sidestep making the mistake of trying to get your child to eat more food. If your child is hungry, she will eat. You also want to avoid mistakenly teaching your child that throwing food is useful at getting you to fight with her, or getting you to feed her. Should your toddler throw food, you can say, "I see that you are finished eating." With no further words, take the food away from the child. Let your actions speak for you. Clean up your child and remove her from the feeding chair. Should she cry, do not respond to the tears or give an additional explanation about why she should not throw food. In this way you allow the logical consequence of her action to teach her that food is not for throwing.

Picky Eater

If meal times have you feeling like a short order cook, it is time to stop catering to your child. It is natural for children to have foods they do not like. Adults have foods they do not care for; why shouldn't children? It is not a help to always serve meals that your child likes. In fact, with new foods it usually takes serving the food at least three different times before a child develops a taste for the food. Unfortunately, many children don't get to that point because Mom or Dad offers to serve them an alternative food.

While the parent means well, fixing a different meal for a child is providing unnecessary service for the child. If your child does not want to eat what is served, then he need not eat. Allow him to discover that he can choose what he will and will not eat. He cannot use his eating habits to control you if you do not react to them. If your child chooses not to eat at all, let him discover the natural consequence of being hungry later. Do not fall into the trap of thinking that your child must eat at every meal. He need not, and very few children actually do eat every meal. When he is hungry, he will eat. If he is not, he won't. We are far more likely to have healthy eaters if we avoid reacting to picky eating habits.

Phone Conversations

Phone conversations can be challenging for many a parent if a child vies for the parent's attention by attempting to interrupt the phone call. Interruptions can take many forms: yelling for a parent, crying, tugging on a parent. Too often the parent caves in and says to the person on the end of the line, "Let me call you back later." This mistakenly teaches the child that she is entitled to a parent's attention whenever she wants it.

A simple solution is to set up a phone call and disconnect so that there is no one on the other end. This allows the parent to ignore the child's demanding misbehavior for as long as it lasts. The child learns that her parent will not be interrupted. Once the misbehavior has stopped, continue to talk for a short time and then end the "call." After a minute or two, walk over to the child as if nothing has happened. This technique may need to be repeated a couple of times but it is helpful for teaching your child that there are times when you may not be interrupted.

Sexual Play Among Children

It is common for a child to engage in exploratory or sexual play at some point in his childhood. It is also common for parents to over-react thereby creating an opportunity for a child to engage in sexual play as misbehavior.

Should your child engage in exploratory play, resist the temptation to place too much value on the behavior. Meet with the child privately and explain to him in a calm voice that everyone's body is private. Explain that private means that what is mine is mine, and what is yours is yours. Your child's body is private, your body is private and other children's bodies are private. Explain to your child that it is not polite to touch another person's body because that invades his or her privacy.

Keep your focus on privacy and personal rights. Do not use judgmental words like "bad" or "wrong." This demeans and discourages the child. Your purpose is to communicate to your child that everyone's body is his or her own. By avoiding lectures on the "badness" or "wrongfulness" of exploratory play you reduce the likelihood that your child will use sexual play to gain unnecessary attention or try to draw you into a power struggle. If your child has a question about body parts, answer as honestly as possible bearing in mind his age.

Following an incident of exploratory play, parents will want to carefully supervise play areas to ensure that play areas are not so isolated as to allow for sexual play. If the exploratory play has occurred at preschool or elementary school ask that the teacher examine his or her classroom and playground setting to make sure that no isolated areas exist and that the teacher carefully monitor play over the next several days to ensure that children do not engage in the play again.

Again, exploratory play is a common developmental stage in children. The goal for the parent is to prevent it from developing into misbehavior. The exception to this would be if your child has engaged in sexual play with an older child. The general rule of thumb is if one child is <u>more than two years of age older </u>than the other child, then the play might be exploitive. In such situations, it is recommended to contact a professional helping resource.

Sibling Rivalry

The purpose of a fight between siblings is usually to draw Mom or Dad into the fight. In the typical sibling fight where a parent intervenes, one child is labeled as the offender while the other is seen as the victim. What Mom or Dad missed was the throwing of the gauntlet by the so-called "victim." It is quite common for younger children to taunt or tease an older sibling into a fight. When the older child hits the younger child, the younger child erupts into tears and wailing. Subsequently, the parent disciplines the older child while the younger child is offered first aid and comfort. Thus it is useful for the younger child to bring a parent into the fight as her ally and often the older child, who feels unfairly treated, lays in wait for an opportunity to get even with his younger sibling.

Parents must be careful to avoid being made into pawns when sibling rivalry occurs. When a child comes up to Mom crying that her brother hit her, Mom can say, "I am sorry that the two of you are having a problem playing together. If someone is unfriendly to me, I choose not to play with him. You may decide to do that as well." Turn a deaf ear to your child's attempts to get you to determine whether she is right or wrong. By refusing to get drawn into the victim's arguments, you make it difficult for her to use fighting to elevate herself. By taking a zero tolerance approach to hurtful behavior you are sending a loud and clear message to your child that fighting is not acceptable.

Should a fight occur in the room with you, you can say, "I see the two of you have decided that you do not wish to get along with each other. I am going to leave since I do not wish to be around unkind behavior." Then leave the room. If you are unable to leave the room, you can say, "I see that the two of you have chosen not to get along with one another. Please leave the room and come back when you are ready to be kind to one another." Your refusal to be a party to their fight reduces the likelihood that either child can use fighting to get your attention or to draw you into a power struggle.

To encourage kind and friendly behaviors in the future make it a habit to "catch" the kids when they are being friendly. When you see your children playing well together say, "The two of you look like you are having such fun together. May I join in the game?" That which we attend to we see again and again. By noting kind behavior and joining in friendly play we teach children the value of friendly and caring behavior.

Profanity

Swearing, or the use of profanity by children can cause the most even-tempered parent to gasp. Children of all ages experiment with profanity. Even children who have parents who don't swear will experiment with it. Naturally, if an adult at home uses profanity, or if the child sees television shows with profanity, the likelihood that he is going to use the words greatly increases. However, keep in mind that your reaction to a child's profanity is what determines whether he will continue to use the words to which you object.

Both the two year old who says "ka-ka" and the four year old who uses a full-fledged obscenity are looking to see how you react. If you gasp or harshly punish your child, you can expect to hear the word again. The first time a child uses inappropriate language say in a friendly, but firm voice, "Honey, I choose not to be around people who use words like that because they are not polite. If you decide to use them, I will move away from you." Then follow up your words with actions and walk away from your child. Actions speak much louder than words. While it can be difficult, particularly in public places, you are better off to turn a deaf ear to profanity. If your child continues to use profanity in a public place, you can explain it is impolite to the other people and if he continues, you will need to leave.

As a way to encourage the development of acceptable words your child can use when he is frustrated, try modeling the use of such words yourself. If you are cut off in traffic while traveling with your child, express your frustration with a statement of fact. "That car is not driving safely!" If you are given to one or two word expletives, try using safe ones like, "Holy Toledo!" If you do slip up and swear in the presence of your child, apologize. Simply say, "I am sorry I said something impolite. It was rude of me and I will work on not doing that anymore." Not only does this acknowledge your mistake, but it also helps reinforce for your child that inappropriate language is not acceptable for anyone to use.

Unnecessary Tears

Some children discover that crying is a useful behavior for getting parents to cave in to their demands. This is referred to as "water power." A loving, but overly sensitive parent can find that in a mistaken effort to prevent their child from experiencing disappointment, she has given the child the mistaken message that she can get her way when she cries.

If your child is crying because she did not get a piece of candy at the store or did not go to a friend's house, have the courage to ignore the tears. From time to time, all individuals will experience a disappointment. If a parent caves in to the tears and buys the candy to pacify the child, or rearranges a schedule so the friend can visit, then the child learns that if she wants something, crying is a useful method for getting it. The child is at risk for concluding that when something is displeasing, Mom or Dad should solve it for her. The next time your child begins to cry when the answer to a request has been "no," be prepared to ignore the tears and take a step back before reacting. If need be, walk away from the child until she has stopped crying.

This same technique can be employed when a child takes a tumble and is clearly not hurt. If a parent rushes in to comfort a child who has fallen, the parent steals from the child the opportunity to learn that if she falls, she has a good person to get her back on her feet, namely, herself. Care must be taken not to overreact to a child's tears. If your child falls and requires no first aid or very little, Mom might try saying, "I see that you took a tumble. You may want to dust yourself off and then you can go back to play." This sends a message of confidence to the child. If first aid is required, then after helping her to put on a bandage you can say, "Looks like you are ready to go back to play." If your child chooses not to, that is fine, but do not let her use continued crying to get you to provide unnecessary comforting. By side-stepping water power, you give your child the opportunity to learn that when she falls, she can count on herself to solve the problem.

Keeping Up With The Joneses

It is not uncommon for children to compare their family to other families. This is something that occurs with many children and in fact, many adults engage in the comparison game. Parents can find themselves engaged in a verbal power struggle if they do not anticipate how to defuse challenges to their good parenting techniques that come in the guise of comparisons to other families or friends.

An example of this might occur when a child is trying to negotiate for a later bedtime. He might say, "Why can't I stay up later? Jerome's parent let him!" Mom and Dad, sensing a need to stop the challenge can make the mistake of trying to explain why they have set the bedtime routine and how it is a help to their son. The child continues to complain that it isn't fair. Mom and Dad repeatedly try to reason with their son and the issue becomes an unpleasant one for all parties involved.

Children can engage in this type of negotiation only if they are successful at getting parents to agree to discuss family issues in the context of how other families raise their children.   A simple and friendly way to avoid "keeping up with the Joneses" is to not take part in the conversation. If your child complains that another family does things differently, have the courage to sidestep the challenge to your parenting by saying, "Every family does things differently. This is what our family does." Continue with whatever you were doing. Do not respond to further comments your child might make to try to get you to negotiate based on comparisons to another family.   This reduces the likelihood that your child can draw you into a power struggle by getting you to defend your decisions.

Temper Tantrums

Nearly all children experiment with temper tantrums at some point in their development. Some children are successful at getting parents to cave in to their demands and learn to use tantrums on a regular basis when they meet with resistance. If this sounds familiar to you, the approach below can help you stop the use of the misbehavior for your child.

On the occasions when you have set a limit for your child, or have said no to her, be prepared to stick to your position. For example, your child asks you if she can paint. You have explained you have company coming over so you cannot set up painting but she is welcome to play with toys in her room or play outside. Your child then decides to scream and flop down on the floor in an attempt to get her way. She is banking on her theatrics to get you to let her have her way. Say nothing, do nothing. Be active. Go about what you were doing. If need be, step over her. Go to another room, moving targets are hard to hit. The tantrum may escalate. Do not be alarmed if your child screams more loudly than usual, or if she throws something. Remember, the goal of her behavior is to get you to cave in to her demands. If screaming louder or throwing things gets you to meet your child's demands, then all you have taught her is that her tantrums will have to be more severe. Stand firm and ignore the tantrum. Let your child discover that once you have said no, you mean it. Let her discover that her tantrums will not get you to change your position.

If your child decides to have a temper tantrum in a public place be prepared to pick her up and leave the place. For example, you and your child want to eat at a fast food place. Prior to going out to eat, say to your child, "Sweetheart, I would like to take you out to eat tomorrow. In the past when we have gone out, you sometimes decide to get angry and scream. If that happens, I will get our food and we will go home. Other people are at the restaurant and it is not polite to ruin their dinner with your screaming. I do not think this will happen, but I wanted you to know that we will have to leave if you forget and decide to get angry". Having stated your position, be prepared to take action. If your child decides to have a temper tantrum when you do not get her a milkshake, be ready to act. With no words at all, take your food and your child and leave the restaurant. The food can be eaten at home. Allow your child to learn that if she wants to go out in public, she must be willing to cooperate and follow the rules that you set.

Tattle-telling

Tattle-telling is an attention seeking behavior. A child who tattles is trying to draw attention to himself by telling Mom or Dad that someone else is doing wrong. Tattle-telling can only work if the child is successful at getting his parent to act on what the child tells him. The best way to defuse tattling is to ask the child in a friendly way, "You wouldn't be tattle-telling would you?" Ask the child the same question each time that he tries to tattle. Be prepared to ask the question four or five times the first time you use this technique. Do not be surprised if your child tells you that you are not listening to him. Just keep asking the same question until the child gives up and walks away. If the child is telling you about a behavior that truly needs your attention, quietly make your way to the problem area and address the problem as though you just happened upon it. Children who tattle are trying to elevate themselves at the expense of another child. In order to stop the use of the behavior parents need to be willing to turn a deaf ear to children who are telling on other children.

Playmates that Fight

Children who frequently play with one another may also frequently fight with one another. This "best of friends, worst of enemies" relationship is one that parents can easily bring to a halt by placing the responsibility for solving the problem with their child.

Parents can meet with their child and the playmate and explain to them that while playing together is fun, fighting is not acceptable. In a friendly voice explain to the children that they are welcome to play with one another, but that if they choose to fight, then it will be a message that today is not a good time for the children to play together. The playmate will be asked to go home and your child will need to stay at home for the rest of the day. They can try again the next day. Explain that if fighting occurs on the following day, the children's play will be postponed for two days.

When the children are playing together appropriately, take time to encourage the positive interaction by coming in and asking them what they are doing. At the end of the play visit, if the day went well, thank both children for their cooperation and invite the playmate back the next day.

Should the play go poorly, do not attempt to referee the fight or solve the problem. Treat both children equally. Remember, it takes two to fight. Let both children discover that if they wish to play together, then they will have to choose not to fight.

Dining Out

Eating out with children can be a pleasant experience provided parents are willing to take time for training. If you find that eating out with your children is unpleasant due to repeated misbehavior, the following technique may be of help to you. Prior to going out to the restaurant, say to your children, "Tonight we are going out to eat. I will need everyone's help to use good manners, speak in a quiet voice in the restaurant, and to stay at the table. That way all of us will be able to enjoy our meal. I don't think that will be a problem for anyone, but if it is we will have to take our food and leave the restaurant." Be completely prepared to take action. When you get to the restaurant, be sure to comment on who is cooperating. For example, "John, you are sitting so nicely at the table. I'm really enjoying eating out with you." Should one of the children misbehave, for instance, bang her silver on the table, say, "Could you help the family out by using your tableware correctly?" If the child refuses or if she misbehaves again, take action. Ask for the food to be boxed up to take with you. Tell your family, "I see that we are not all ready to eat out in a restaurant. We can try this again on another day, but we will need to leave now so we do not disturb the other people." Then leave. Do not let a child's promises to behave or a child's temper tantrum stop you from taking action. Let your actions speak for you.

If both parents are present, you can alter the above approach in the following way. Prior to going out, explain to your children, "Tonight we are going out to eat. Your Dad and I will need everyone's help to use good manners, speak in a quiet voice in the restaurant, and to stay at the table. That way all of us will be able to enjoy our meal. I don't think that will be a problem for anyone, but if it is your Dad or I will take home whoever chooses to misbehave and the rest of the family will stay to finish their meal."

Don't be surprised if everyone chooses to cooperate when you first use this technique. It may not be until the next meal out that a child misbehaves. Be prepared to follow through at that time. While it is not pleasant to take a screaming or crying child out of a restaurant, it is far more unpleasant to find that you cannot go out to a restaurant with your family. Taking time to train your child pays for itself in the long run.

Intentional Destruction

Sometimes when a child decides to have a temper tantrum, he will break something in his anger. Whether the object is broken because the child threw it or kicked it, the damage occurred because the child chose to use his temper to force his parents to cave in to his demands. If this is happening with your child, here is a helpful suggestion. At a neutral time, meet with your child and say, "Sometimes when you are angry you decide to throw and kick things. On a couple of occasions you have broken things when you were angry. For instance, you threw the ball when you did not want to come for dinner and the garage window was broken. Your Mom and I hope that you decide not to use your temper when you are angry, but we also realize that if you do decide to use your temper and break things, it will be your responsibility to pay for the item you break. We will have the same rule for your Mom and I. If we break something because we are angry, we will have to replace the item with our money."

Then next time your child breaks something in anger, wait until the tantrum is over and then meet with your child. Tell him the cost of the item and ask for the money. If the child does not have the money, he can repay it with his allowance. Take care to speak in a calm and respectful voice. Your goal in using this approach is for your child to discover two facts. First, that breaking things in anger will not get you to cave in to his demands. Second, you want him to learn that a logical consequence of destroying things is the responsibility for replacing them. Use care not to be punitive. Let the consequence speak for itself.

Homework

One of the first challenges parents of elementary school children face is how the homework issue will be addressed. Many parents make the mistake of becoming "homework police" and find that the job is not only thankless but usually futile. Well-intentioned parents try to "make" their child do her homework only to find themselves in a ferocious fight with their child. If this sounds familiar, don't despair. Instead, try the following suggestion.

Meet with your child at a neutral time. Say to your child, "Honey, I've been acting as though I have to make you do your homework. I realize that is a mistake. Your homework is your business and is between you and your teacher. You may decide to complete it at the child care center, or you may decide to complete it at home. If you don't get it finished at the center, you can work on it between 7:00 and 8:00 because I will be free to answer any questions you have about it. If you complete it at the center, then you and I will have that time to go for a bike ride or play a game together. If you decide not to do your homework, I guess you'll have to explain that to your teacher the next day."

Then let your actions speak for you. The following day at 7:00 p.m. ask your child if she completed her homework. If she says yes, offer to look it over for accuracy and then say, "Looks like you understood what your teacher taught you. What would you like to do together?" If she says she has not completed her homework you might say, "Do you understand what your teacher wants you to do?" Provided she does, say, "Okay, then you can work on this in your room. If you need my help, just call me."

Keep in mind that your child may go into her room and choose to play rather than complete her homework. If your child does not do her homework, do not save her from the consequences. Her teacher has already explained to her what happens when her homework is incomplete. Adlerians have known for a long time that the best way to teach responsibility to a child is by giving it to her. We can best help our children take on the responsibility of homework by placing the task in their hands, rather than ours.

Poor Sportsmanship

An important part of all children's development is learning to play sports. Just as important as learning how to play sports, is learning good sportsmanship. This is an area where a parent can greatly help a child. As your child begins to play sports, he will discover that part of playing a game is losing a game. Some children choose to become angry when this occurs. It is the responsibility of a parent to intervene when this occurs.

Take for instance the playing of a family basketball game. As you and your child play, if he chooses to get angry at performing poorly you can stop the game. Say in a calm voice, "I am happy to play with you, but I will not play if you decide to get angry because then the game is no longer fun." Let your child make the next move. If he chooses to return to a friendly game, then continue to play. If he continues to get angry when he plays poorly, then stop playing the game. Your child can continue to play the game on his own, but it will be without you. This quietly, but firmly lets your child know that the playing of sports is to be fun.

Another sign of poor sportsmanship is repeated allegations of unfairness. If your child is playing a game with friends and you hear him repeatedly complaining that his friends cheat, your child may be attempting to elevate himself at the expense of his friends. He may have mistakenly concluded that he should always perform the best in a game. Offer the following idea to your child and then stop talking. Say, "If you do not enjoy playing ball with your friends, you can always decide to stop playing the game." Do not allow your child to draw you into a discussion of how his friends cheated. This gives your child the chance to excuse himself from good sportsmanship-like behavior.

Help encourage sportsmanlike behavior by commenting on how your child's team worked together during a game. Make a point during group sports to compliment other players on their game. When playing the game yourself, thank another player for helping you during the game. Notice how your child and another team member assist one another during a game. This helps teach your child the value and necessity of playing as a team rather than trying to be a star.

Walk to the Window Moments

Parenting takes patience and forethought, and yet even with a sound parenting philosophy, challenges to good child rearing techniques will occur. An excellent method for reducing the likelihood that misbehavior is made useful to a child is "walking to the window."

Simply put, this means taking a moment to turn away and gather your thoughts before you react to your child. Knee-jerk reactions to a child's behavior very often are not the best approach to a problem. Children will say and do things that are designed to get a parent involved with them. Prior to taking action parents are well served by asking themselves, "Is this a behavior that I want to see again?" If it is not, then a good rule of thumb is to refrain from comment or action. Much of what parents want to accomplish with their child can best be accomplished by not responding to misbehavior.

"Walking to the window" also helps parents avoid calling upon their anger in order to defeat or punish a child. Individuals call upon their anger to give them permission to say and do things that they would not ordinarily say or do. A child who is trying to get her parent to cave in to a temper tantrum may say some extremely unpleasant things. It is very important for a parent to walk away and then return to the situation when the parent's goal is to help rather than to defeat or punish the child.

From time to time a child may also do something that is extremely funny and yet is not a behavior a parent would like to see again. To avoid giving unnecessary attention to the behavior, this parent will need to take a moment to look away or walk away until the urge to laugh passes.

Every parent will make child-rearing mistakes. By taking a moment to stop and reflect before reacting to a child's behavior, parents give themselves the opportunity to make an informed decision about their next step thereby reducing the likelihood of a mistake. Remember, one of the most beautiful qualities of human beings is that we absolutely have the freedom to choose our attitude towards every situation we experience.

The Courageous Parent

Raising a child can be one of the most significant contributions a person can make to society. The outcome can be helpful or hurtful. It takes great courage and strength on the part of a parent to pave the way for the child to develop into a socially interested member of society.

Mistakes will be made. That means that from time to time, every parent will need to look for a technique to correct a child rearing error. This presents more of a challenge for some people than others. A common mistake occurs when a parent decides he will try a new child rearing technique. The word "try" implies failure. When implementing a new technique, a parent needs to bear in mind that he is teaching his child a new behavior. Just as it took time for the child to learn to misbehave, it will also take time for the child to learn that the misbehavior no longer works.

It is not uncommon for a child's behavior to worsen when a parent initially uses a new technique. Do not allow yourself to become discouraged if this occurs. It is an indication that the child is trying even harder to get you to respond to his misbehavior. Should you make the mistake of giving in, you have mistakenly taught your child to misbehave more steadfastly and for a lengthier period of time.

Once a parent has determined that he or she has been making misbehavior useful to the child and that a new approach is needed, it is very important that the parent also firmly decides to follow through with the new approach he or she will use in response to the child's misbehavior. Choose a technique to stop the use of the misbehavior and look for many opportunities to deliberately encourage cooperative and responsible behavior. Recognize that the courageous parent takes action to ensure that his or her child develops into a responsible and cooperative member of society who cares about the welfare of fellow human beings.

Suggested Readings

Dreikurs, Rudolf, and Soltz, Vicki. **Children: The Challenge.** New York: Plume Penguin Group, 1990.

Walton, Francis X., and Powers, Robert L. **Winning Children Over: A Manual for Teachers, Counselors, Principals and Parents.** Columbia, SC: Adlerian Child Care Books. 2006